LID
AND
SPOON

ALBERTA T. TURNER

Lid & Spoon

University of Pittsburgh Press

Published by the University of Pittsburgh Press, Pittsburgh, Pa. 15260
Copyright © 1977, Alberta T. Turner
All rights reserved
Feffer and Simons, Inc., London
Manufactured in the United States of America

Library of Congress Cataloging in Publication Data

Turner, Alberta T.
  Lid and spoon.
  (Pitt poetry series)

  I. Title.
PS3570.U66L5   811'.5'4   77-73470
ISBN 0-8229-3357-8
ISBN 0-8229-5284-X pbk.
ISBN 0-8229-3362-4 lim. ed.

Acknowledgment is made to the following publications for permission to re-print poems that appear in this book: *Cleveland Anthology, Dark Tower, Grove, Heartland II, The New Review, Pocket Pal, Stand,* and *Three Rivers Poetry Journal.*

"Houses Trot Toward Us" originally appeared in the *Poetry in Transit* project, both in a booklet and on bus placards, as "Elm Street". Copyright © 1976 by the Poets' League of Greater Cleveland. Reprinted by permission of the League.

*The publication of this book is supported by a grant
from the National Endowment for the Arts
in Washington, D.C., a Federal agency.*

TO S.L.H. 1913–1973

This is not a book on how to make it happen,
it will happen.

These are ways of having it

with bread and without
square and round

lid and spoon.

CONTENTS

LID
AND
SPOON

Understand:

when I picked up the frog
the skin came off,
when the mare trotted by and I grabbed the mane
it came out in tufts,

your face smeared.

These are instead.

WRISTS

Asked me to be a woman:
           didn't mind
           swelled
           grew fine hair
           (you can braid fine hair to hang an anvil on)
           oiled my hands.

Asked me to make a god:
           couldn't do it.
           God was already grease
           a warm grease shaped like a rug you could
           stand on and be gone.

Asked for bread:
           couldn't do that either.
           So I said that bread was doom. I said their gums
           were sore and I rubbed
           their gums.

Then they asked how it felt to lean:
           so I took them one tide forward and one
           tide back, showed them that rock was red only
           if wet, showed how cattle doubled when they stood
           knee-deep, how the fence went back as far as
           the road, and grass
           was salt.

"Kinder," they begged,
           so I put on socks
           and felt for the ground through moss,
           showed them how fish spit out my hook,
           and how, when I lay under fish, they gaped
           and waved.

Then they grinned and shook and broke my hands off.

How explain to the finned a narwhal drowned? To the hoofed a sand dollar split?

So I offered wrists and they took
my wrists.

Get My Collar:

it's young leather,
I punched the holes myself.

A chain claps the flagpole, chain drags
from the axle, I'm holding a chain,

and a collar grows stiff without grease.

EMILIO, ROMERO, FATHER, CHESTER, TED —

Sex was curling your hair and standing outfield
till the ball went by and you were looking the other way.
It was cleaning the cat's box while Mother
delivered the kittens — holding a sick fur in your lap
until it grew stiff and covered
with flies.

It was three women and Father on Sundays:
trying to stay awake for a good-night kiss —
being quiet on Christmas morning — hating your sister
if he spoke to her first.

And Emilio, who never learned English,
who wore a white coat and liked to carry little girls
with his hand in their crotch — and Romero,
who built the stone wall and crooned all day
in Italian — and Dr. Robinson, who, when you couldn't
swallow, said you had no sore throat — and Grandfather
asking for hot water on his shredded wheat and feeling
too unwelcome to come out of his room and
preferring the Odd Fellows Home.

It was women who moved in our house.
Men were hired and pleased.

So I praise Ted (his eyes are near together) —
I tell Sam only the kindest lies — I bring Art
dry jokes — save blown fuses for Brent — put
lettuce in Leonard's sandwich — ask Chester
about roses —

We People

have to die to make room.
Imagine your face full of sandy socks!

Once dead, we have plenty of seats
in Austrian-pine cones.

We are loved as we love a fistful of poppy seeds —
all silky   and don't need names.

Sal must be here and Dumby and
all Mother's salmon-pink, white-eyed phlox.

Something heaves, something pulls down.
When my spoon sticks in a gravy of saints,

I know that riding the waterdrops down from the spout
and splashing up before they reach the drain

come spoons that will stir it again.

WEIGHT

Lay the crumbs parallel,
lay the pebbles parallel,
lay the blocks parallel,
can you lift the next one?

❋

A dappled flank presses down
the moss and pebbles and prickers I live in
and you and all our pets —
a damp flank — we guess the hock;
the tail doesn't flick;
it must be asleep.
This animal is dreaming us.

❋

Weight hanged the man:
the gallows had no need of him,
the loop held its own sides apart.

Sky squat, feathers fluffed out:
hen rid of the egg,
egg rid of the chick.

❋

I am a spool, you are a spool,
we are a pull.
If you jerk, I dizzy; if I spin, you hum;
if you stop, I loop over myself and knot.

❋

Suppose
there were no selves,
that fingers pulled for thumbs' sakes
and toes climbed backs
to rest backs?
Suppose ears
strained sounds through combs

and sun, pressing ears through steam,
talked of such service?

Ash does seem
to fall.

FOUR SURVIVORS

I

It's not being woman.
The wreck was *helmed,* not *manned.*

Not woman, but orifice,
bowl with a hole, amphora
and weight:
　　to feel water
　　into your mouth
　　down through your throat without swallowing
　　your pelvis just
　　emptying —
married to that.

II

I was all right
as long as they told me so:
　　the braided rope, leaves edged with drops,
　　enough mica in the sand.
But all night the pluck, pluck,
pluck —

Small wonder the suitors went for the wine and flocks
and gagged Telemachus,
who tried to tell them
his mother really wove,

or that Odysseus waited as long as he could
before taking on all that wool.

III

A fish head nibbled the pier,
the boats had been gone since four,
an ant climbed my pants cuff
and fell off.

So I put it together the way it *ought* to be:
Cassandra divined a fish head,
cackled down toward the cove
and spotted me, and picked her teeth.
I asked for Agamemnon.
She said, "He's taking a bath,
but go on up."

IV

You say I survive.
Did you know my mother ripped lace off my slips
because it scratched?

My smooth chin, greasy with cream,
my heavy boughs, propped with sticks,
somebody's grandmother's silk-and-velvet crazy quilt
leaking out
            under a lean-to,
                    the featherstitching intact.

This Room Is Full of Things I Know

the names of:
bowls of blood
door frames
combs   pots of chives
tea strainers and square tin boxes
of loose tea.

I'm told to choose
flutter over one tea   then another
crouch in the strainer
comb the chives
back away from a bowl

back squeaking into a door frame
upside down.

FORBIDDING MOURNING

(for A.T.)

You want so much to go, plan it in such detail
that finally we want it too.
You pack and unpack and repack your bag.
In the end you leave it behind.

I wish you'd taken the bag.

What shall we do with Prue's polar-bear-in-a-globe
that you shook every time you passed
to make it snow?
Or my early Christmas card of a fox
that rears back from its paw in a trap?

We can bury you in the only jacket
you ever had made.

But how can we use three big reading glasses?

Or a blue/brown cup marked "Cheshire Cheese,"
that holds two paperclips and a stretched rubber band
and the stem of a fig?

Such Comfort, Soup:

grain you can strip,
cement block soft as potato buds,
skin swollen to pap.

When you bite on hard, it's china
or bone splinter — and you stop.

IN A NAME

The boy died.
She was to have been the second son,
with his father's second name,
after little Uncle Albert, who drowned
one Sunday when he was supposed to be in church,
and before him, the Prince Consort.

If it weren't for that vulgar name,
she could leave the soft
brat on the bus. But as it is,
it has to be dried, fed,
apologized —
✿
Maker of this universe,
if you give this page a name, do you
risk
    an ankle bracelet
    a tattoo
    a strawberry mark
if you write at the bottom
    John or Finn or
    Bernadette?
✿
Opened all the cans and found them
full — none shriveled,
none green —
careful canisters
full dreams.
The merchants lift and tie,
ring an honest till.
If they knew what I came for they'd
have the name.

So they take me along the shelves:
"this for cats
this for after nine
this for tired seams."

They show me bins,
rows of beans and corn,
and on the far wall, scorched,
the cans with no names.
These are already warm.
These will do.

Houses Trot Toward Us,

some have stars on their foreheads.
They trot porch to porch, screen doors snapping,
shades lowering and lifting.
Just out of reach they toss their eaves,
lower their front steps, and begin to graze.

HOOD   BUTTON   SHELL   FUR

Gravity and wind   so   bells
feet in pairs ring pant legs
sausage curls clang hoods
domes hunch on traffic lights that lift
and swing

also cold   its squirrel tail   its nose drop
and cannon mouths   their coin

❋

One slave
to fasten the clasp of her cross
one
to slice her butter onto her toast

And she is fatherless
fed the bully to the meanest hog
sewed his buttons on a girl's coat

❋

Assume
that custard is smooth
that blue is sad and kind

Assume a god
ladle of fish
ladle of glue

And why not perch the snail shell on the log
as if the snail were still climbing out?

❋

Three beans in a row   red beans
three snows with no salt between
Ladder perhaps?

"Stop" And I would
But without wheels? Without road?
Stop an axe   drop a hand

And fur is as angry   as I can   today

GREECE: A SEARCH FOR SALT

I

Came for goats
and orange peel under a cannon,
and to ask if a bald hill could still green grapes
and if any olive trees remembered Christ.

Came to taste if the wine-dark sea
was salt.

II

Poseidon's temple has no roof.
Wearing white coveralls, he pushes a cart —
ices on sticks and fresh-squeezed orange juice.
"Kilroy," "Byron," and a blurred "Tucker 1774."
He's repaired his columns; no danger of falling rock.

Poseidon's hair is pepper and salt.
He squats down: the bay of Sounion is flat;
two yachts and a pedal catamaran
anchor and tread.
French is spoken, German-English-Swedish is spoken
on his porch. Poseidon is content.

III

Cretan woman milks a goat,
rides an ass sideways, legs banging the ribs,
scrubs clothes in a wheelbarrow,
dries grapes on the roof,
puts a child on the bus, kisses it, gets off.

In September cornstalks and sunflower heads dry.
She doesn't cut them.
She crosses herself four times when she passes a church,
loads a donkey with firewood, melons, her husband,
grins and strides ahead
or strides behind.

IV

Push a rock up   out of the sea
four hundred feet   six hundred.
Whiten   let crumble.

When the gods change, ring that rock with teeth,
rake that sea with stone shot,
mound larger stones to hutch the new god.
Lichen   wait.

When the gods change again, allow ants
to bring rugs and lace and cylindrical beads,
breed mules to carry their fat grubs up.
Shore the first temple (these grubs are full of milk),
board up weak arches, pile cannonballs out of reach.
Wait.
The gods are not changing yet.
You may lick that rich melt.

V

We older women
squat on the quay on folded blankets
and wrap our heads in black to just above the chin.
At Amorgos we are lifted on deck
in our own chair.

At Kos our bundle flies open and our
long stiff drawers fly out.

We hold a bag of pears: three each for the ladies,
four, six   till they spill.
Two drachmas? Four? We throw the money back.

At the airport, our mustache is gray.
When a child cries, we look past.

VI

So, if you've come to Delphi for the oracle, remember,
Christians have climbed the rock above it
and climbed off,
olive stumps give small, pointed olives,
earth has quaked.

Rows of hips rim the Castalian spring,
but the oracle is stuck on an unambiguous word,
something between a mouse in a candy wrapper
and a green linnet with a streak, like
a slit   on the side of its throat.

When the Sink

swirls and swallows the bead,
please, no rungs.

ANYONE, LIFTING

Someone's hiding in the graveyard:
police car across the drive, helicopter
above. Dogs are staked.

Someone is hiding here, mint in his sleeves,
full length on a stone, ears flared out.

And something is missing.

They want a man in a crouch, a woman with
hair over her eyes, anyone   lifting.

DAUGHTER, DAUGHTER

When you peel an egg, leave the skin.
If you jump rope, drop the loop.
A pound of feathers equals a pound
of axes.

Blackbirds don't make good pies.
Fill a fruit pie twice as full.
Tin coughs, glass gargles, sand swallows.

Steal only what you can wear.
Two nickles don't ring like a dime.
Saints come in pints, quarts, gallons.

Step on a crack, break your mother's back;
skip one, break your own.

Seeds are round.
Shells listen.

THE FLOODING

They couldn't take the rock
that got so hot you had to fold your coat
under your shorts
or the hoof mark
that sun baked till it held water.

They took jelly jars and lids
and most hens.

And the pond?
that flat August top — burry
with dust prongs?

Or did it flood from under,
lift porches on long stems,
settle hills — like eye, beak, tuft of comb —
plump hen
on her dust bath?

PRETEND

Pretend the four sitting opposite are dogs
with filmed eyes and paralyzed paws.
Their hocks have thick calluses and no sleeves.
Pretend the long faces, the snub faces,
the string of drool, the escaped fang
licked back under the lip.
The bus lurches   a tail slips out.

Pretend the child,
tube in his neck, tube in his arm.
Pull the crib sides up
as if he would crawl. Hang a squirrel
from the lamp. Roll his eyelids back.
He'll grow, this one. In six years
he'll laugh. You'll prop him
on the seat beside you. He'll point
and squeal. You'll lift and
carry him sideways off the bus,
a little slower this time. He's getting fat.

And pretend
the woman walking toward us
down the hospital corridor,
her white iron staff as tall as she is,
her I-V swinging from it, the loop
taped to her nose.
Her robe tents, her feet slush out, she
comes   she   comes

Pretend a wedge   a whole sky   of her

SCIENCE

My paws are flippers. They were hands two hours ago, then paws. I was slicing an onion. I thought *I* cried, but then I heard the onion, little gulps. So I did the water ritual and the salt, but it still kept gulping — all through the stew. When I spooned for it, my hands were paws and wouldn't hold the spoon.

I thought if I made no fuss, maybe they'd grow back. But now flippers. I'm scared. We live twelve miles from the lake, and Niagara Falls and the Ship Canal are between me and the sea. I've seen seals humping over rocks. I couldn't make it to the sea.

And all because I cut the wrong onion in a hundred thousand onions, because someone cut this onion's great, great, greatest onion with a charmed knife.

I'm drawing my flipper across the same knife, over the stew. The onion has stopped sobbing. The left flipper's not hard to do. If the left paw grows back, I'll slice the right.

Don't Say

I'm smart for a woman, smart as a man,
say   I mated a fox   and my whelps run
bushy and sharp and a beautiful shade of red.

"WE CAN USE WHAT WE HAVE
TO INVENT WHAT WE NEED"

(A. Rich)

For example, *wing:*

>   when we're heavy, a flap;
>   when we're thin, a hook;
>   when we're sad,

✿

To be sad is to fire a shot
that lodges one pellet under a tail
or ankles that bulge over double-A shoes
or tires where someone has planted mint.

I think of the man who picked through
can after curbside can. When police emptied him,
they found an unhatched egg and the skeleton
of a one-year-old boy.

He claimed he had to finish them.

✿

"A chick will take the first thing its sees for its mother."
Then how keep from seeing
the cheek of the water pitcher,
the belly of the chest of drawers?
A blanket hovers my foot,
two Kleenex I squeezed last night
breathe in and out.

Mother, curtains loop your square mouth,
branches jerk and poke.
Mother, in decency, suck in your teeth.

✿

An axe to grind is only a lump,
but tall spruces shiver like bliss
when an axe hums toward a smithy.

✿

If I open my eyes, I'll see wing marks on the ceiling.
All night tremolo and thud
and long stops to preen.
The screen door rang, a whirring sucked
hair off my arm, then powdered my skin.

This morning the room hangs straight from its chain.

LONG LOWING

The stone farms in Belgium and Brittany,
shaped like coats: the parents
in the center house, the sons
built against it, the stone channel
brimming suds.

You want to go in, left, under the eaves,
and put your head
between stanchions.

BODY OF —

Feet of clay begin below the knee
like wet socks.
Drying, they arch,
dry, they ache.

The hand of chance folds over its thumb.
Feeling for mouths,
it fingers necks.

The stroke of doom always smooths back
the eye it squeezed out.

The face of truth is bald, with a pulse
and possible ears.
Eyelids rolled back, it stares.

The body of my knowledge has no joints,
counts and keeps counting its legs
and feeling itself for wings.

JANE

You ask how I know I'm a woman
now that my womb is gone
my son grown
my husband blind.

You ask if I *am* a woman.
Have I planted fish under my corn?
Do I sleep curled on my side?
How big is my ball of string?

But suppose I don't say
my shovel's notched like an axe
and if my skull were boiled with yours
you couldn't tell from the teeth?

My son is feeding his baby.
I lock the house for the night.
He slides me a place on the bed
and lays his son in my lap.

A hand like a lip asleep,
and a fist like a lifted face,
if Mother had said it was all right,
they could touch me   anywhere.

I DOUBT THAT YOU
CAN COMFORT THINGS

I
Lava:
puddle that slumps
and spreads and steams —
Every thing it breathes on
catches fire or goes limp,
till it thickens, cools,
cuts every knee
that applies.

II
Earthquake
didn't mean;
it dropped.
A great tray or bowl loved it,
filled, grunted, let it settle itself.
Allowed skitters, allowed sticks
to grow and be fitted, stones
to crack and be cemented,
and another shrug or tilt —

III
Leaf
at the end of a twig
drags in the river.
Leaf is green,
river is water.
River spins it — and jerks,
spins back — and jerks.
Should be teased off,
is not teased off.
Is washed.

IV

Wind,
if you're my brother,
why rip between my two
dearest teeth, leaving them filed
and distrusting each other?
Why take my salt and my water?
Brother, I've hired bees for the afternoon,
paid for a room, and found you a tower
with four stretched arms.

V

Dark
is frightened if you
haven't built a house behind it or
strung a clothesline to it or
taken its arm.
But you need to pour out light
to find the cup.

VI

Wood
tells of sawing, planing, boxing,
then of cold and weight —
that for beginning.
Only long after, admits
the lift, the loose box cored and arched —

But there are signs:
a log burning and after burning,
no phoenix bird, but the wood gone out.

Do I Dip

my pitcher
in a pintable well?

ACCOUNTING

Twenty of them. Count:
five with heads
eight with holes
seven of some soft stuff —

You put boots on the cat,
a diamond bracelet on the crow.
Look at yourself grinning out of the spider web,
stuffiing your twins into a pouch.

Two of you have identical spoons,
four go to the same shelf for salt,
three return to the fifth stone from the door
to tie your shoes.

A dried bee crunches underfoot.
Two of you will crunch bees.

SPOUT

This morning wheels by for my approval:
a stalk of dock, tinkling with seeds,
two stray wheats sawing a log,
a waterfall in strings.
A flag lifts as it passes, a windsock
dips. I could be God.

So I've boiled a kettle of leeks
and broken a brick and held my hand
under a spout.
I've pulled a stalk off a rhubarb and
another stalk off another rhubarb.

And when I find a pump in the middle of a field
and it has no handle,
and thirty feet from the road I find a stone
with a lilac on either side,
I know that I must have been
and may, even now, be
God.

TENERIFFE

Living halfway up
(the trucks go up in first gear
and back in first gear),
the almond trees bare,
fog, two sweaters, babushka,
the terrace stones wet —

Below, you know: bananas, camels, the ocean —
Above, you know: pines, desert, a hole
that smokes, that you could cook a fish on —

For now, one terrace for grass,
one terrace for tilth,
one cow to plow,
one calf.

If Face

is a locust cracking its shell
or a snake wriggling out of its skin
or a polliwog,

what pokes through first?

Not nose, still flat, not tongue
still testing to see if mouth has roof,
nor eye, stuck shut.

More likely breath, steaming
like a good pudding,
fusing
the east, the right, the top, the
rest.

Paper

is for wrapping fish
and layering cups
and lining shoes.

When I Was Small

someone told me I was a girl.
Was that good?
Well, it wasn't wrong.
I took the bottle from my baby sister
to feed my doll. That was wrong.

Father had shoes, Mother had shoes,
we had shoes. The cat had kittens.
Some of them were girls. Father came home
after supper; he was cold. On Sundays
the lawnmower broke.

Jesus was a boy, Santa was a boy,
but they were one of a kind.
Dr. Doolittle went to the moon, but
Dorothy went to Oz, and the Dutch Twins
were one of each.

Then I found the cat in the bathroom,
with two still lumps and squeezing out a third,
and I squeezed my eyes and felt for the door and
never told.

"THIS DREAM THE WORLD IS HAVING ABOUT ITSELF"

(Wm. Stafford)

One foot on the center of a top, it leans
away from the top's lean,
then leaps off toward the top's tilt
in a drift so light it spikes
on grass and pennyroyal.

It dreams a cloud whose paws scrabble and slip,
whose tail breaks off in a splash of rain,
and a man riding the tip of a hooked beak,
gauging its wind, foretelling its weather,
and swelling with pride when it unhooks
and flaps up to another branch.

The fledgling upside-down under the pine
it didn't dream.
Imagine inside the world's eye:
shelves — most of them empty,
stairs — none of them clean,
on one shelf a claw, on one a wing,
a bird on one —

"We are all gestures the world makes,"
but, world, whose turtle I tip on its back,
whose asparagus I tilt into its mouth,

am I flung up against a green branch let fly?

A Pointed Arch — Any Stone,

I have no gift
for glass.

SISTERS

There were always five
                    or three or seven
cut out of brown paper
and joined at the skirt or curls,
with the same nose, the same lunch
pail. They had separate beds, but the same
lunch.

Being one, you took little things,
her seat next the teacher, *her* turn.
You put them back, but you owed.

If you tripped, one hauled you up;
if you died, you left them your babies, your old
cat, Mother's knives. But mostly
you stood
while one pinned.

HOOP

If you feel up
and pull to the right
as if you heard rings slide along a rod,
you can shut off the sun.

"Be honest,"
but every time I count the fingers of one hand
they joint.

Ant poison is sweet,
the closet door sticks.
When I grab it, you point to the child.
Must I account for all three?

"It's terminal: a virus, a fungus, or
Hodgkin's disease. Imagine
lying there knowing it's terminal!
And she just says she's bored!"
Woman, do you know your toe ends
completely before the end of your shoe?
And that you just drove over the most
enormous cucumber Hecuba ever raised?
Of course she's bored.

Spear a small ring — and you bracelet your wrist.
Spear a big ring — and you hug your spear to you
and snap it against your eye.

White Sound

is what you hear
to keep from hearing.

Rock music in the dress shop
chatters at tags.

If you hear the clop, clop of a horse cop,
the light is red.

The deaf are not warned: white cats
are always the first run over.

The chink of trays down the hospital corridor —

The light snore —

FOUND ON A WOMAN
HANGING UP A RAINCOAT

In her right hem a pinch of wool
and half a movie ticket
(the night God came as a large spider
out of a wall in Sweden
and she left the headlights on).

On her right palm a lump.
(She squeezed the scissors till they broke;
the house had no roof
but she pulled the damper down;
outside, sand dipped and ran toward Iceland.)

In her cuff a thumb.
(Indian graves at Whitehorse,
doghouse over each grave —
but why the bullet holes?)

Name of a Home in Vermont,
long talk with a very old cat,
two hours helping a baby breathe — and
windshield wipers, windshield wipers —

PROVERBS, RIDDLES, SPELLS

I
Bellies are round, puppies are round,
the moon is round
if you fork her in a tree.

Any girl can be a spindle.

If frogs were princes, if horses
wishes — would you, beggar lady,
horse a frog?

Find a loop. Is it ring size?
Neck size?

II
A whiff of sage, a plop of grease,
a pinch of salt — three women
and a crib.

Don't overfeed the jackal. Remember
what stinks.

III
Half a broom swept a porch; half a
broom twitched in a corner; half
a broom rode off under a skirt.

Are you cold enough to burn your finger?

IV

If the table's set with silver,
there'll be a basket in the center.
If the table's set with gold,
the soup will be thin and cold.
If the table's set with lead,
there'll be a barrel at the head.

But if the meat is on the wood —?

V

Three strings hang out of the teapot,
three little paper tags.

VI

A can, a bottle, and a jug
soaked off each other's names.
The can has hiccups, the bottle's
got a prune stuck in her throat,
the jug's down by the ferry
making change.

VII

Put a dog to sleep and bay the moon,
put a boy to sleep and skip a stone,
put a man to sleep and
mow a farm.

EIGHT

(for T.S.)

On the first branch a ball,
a greasy black tennis ball —
soft, with a sort of hair growing off it.

On the next branch a leg
wedged into the crotch,
a gray leg;
I climb around it.

The third branch is smooth,
the fourth bald,
the fifth dead.
It snaps off when I spring
up, to grab the sixth,
which holds a fur
that snarls when the branch dips
and leaps on my chest.
I carry the fur.

The top branch holds a seat,
a sort of basket laced
by four sprays of twigs.
The fur and I rest.
The fur sleeps.
And I could sleep:
leaves sliver and plate us,
we are limber here and lifted,

but after seven comes eight.
I grab two loops of light
and climb off.

PRONOUN SONG:
TRYING TO GET USED TO A DEATH

(for S. L. H.)

By now you've sorted out
what you like (nothing I'd choose).
I've never been so simple
to any one.

But I still want to shock you:
    I don't like fruit.
    I never run unless I have to.
    I believe you're still around, though you don't
    want me to and I don't know
    when you listen.

I saved your clothespins.
I won't water your geraniums.
I wish you weren't dead.

I mean
        eels in your trees, strawberries
under your bed.

But I also said *spoons* and *good morning-
glory* to you.

Yesterday I said *are*
and *is*.
   ✦
You tugged the vine down from the pigeon's nest
to square the brick again
(the eggs were empty that year).
My bottom was sore from one hard chair.

Time to walk the railroad track
to hunt cartridges between the ties,
to run our hands along the rail
and bring them off red.

*

Dreamed the anger of wood grain,
the need for up, but lay
under holes in the roof, humped
my back to any push,
my face going *wah, wah* toward any
streak of wet.

Then dreamed the rightness of saw and
plane — your raw ends hissed as they
ripped across — tongue squirmed into groove
and stuck — you drank screws — spun
and stood, a perfect leg (on one
bent nail you screamed).

*

To name it is to pitch tents
and corner squares.
Mist won't stay hooked to a spruce,
or the tomato swell red
without its stem.

To have it, we have to name it, Sal.
Perhaps a basketful will stand
for that rough hood
you jammed over us
last June.

*

I came round under the bushes
and looked in — your nightdress was pulled
down — your smell
and your huge red foot pushed me out.
One of our jokes: "Take care,
you wouldn't want me to find
your mortal remains."

First   clean hooves
second   queer pains
third   square cars
fourth   fat loaves
fifth   queer pains
sixth   tight lids
seventh   queer pains
eighth   deep spoons.

PITT POETRY SERIES

Paul Zimmer, General Editor

*T*HIS first edition of

LID AND SPOON

consists of two thousand copies

in paper cover, five hundred copies

hardbound in boards,

and fifty specially bound copies

numbered and signed by the author.